UTHMAN BIN 'AFFAN

(Allah be pleased with him)

The Third Caliph of Islam

Compiled by
'ABDUR RAHMAN SHAD

Revised by
PROF. 'ABDUL HAMEED SIDDIQ1

KITAB BHAVAN
New Delhi-110002 (INDIA)

KITAB BHAVAN
1784, Kalan Mahal, Darya Ganj,
New Delhi-1100 02
Phone : 91-11-23277392/93, 23274686
Fax : 91-11-23263383
Email : nasri@vsnl.com
Website : www.kitabbhavan.com

Edition 2005

ISBN : 81-7151-363-8

Laser Typesetting at :
T.J. Enterprises
Pataudi House, Darya Ganj,
New Delhi-1100 02 (India)

Published by :
Nusrat Ali Nasri for Kitab Bhavan
1784, Kalan Mahal, Darya Ganj,
New Delhi-1100 02 (India)

Printed in India at :
Lahooti Fine Art Press
1711, Suiwalan,
New Delhi-1100 02 (India)

فَسَيَكْفِيكَهُمُ اللّٰهُ ۚ وَهُوَ السَّمِيعُ الْعَلِيمُ ﴿١٣٧﴾ ط

And Allah will suffice thee (for defence) against them. He is the Hearer, the Knower.

(Al Baqrah : 137)

CONTENTS

FOREWORD

This book which is the third part of the Series, is a biography of Hadhrat 'Uthman bin 'Affan (Allah be pleased with him) and his remarkable achievements in the history of Islam.

Every attempt has been made to narrate only authenticated facts in a clear, concise and lucid style.

May this book serve the purpose for which, it has been written.

M. A. QAZI,

U.P.M.,
Dhahran (Saudi Arabia)

PREFACE

The period preceding the advent of Islam was the dark age of ignorance during which the Arabs had been accustomed to idolatry, gambling and drinking. They were quite ignorant of the rudiments of social virtues. The country was rent into innumerable petty states which were always at war with one another. Trifling disputes between individuals would lead to a terrible conflagration and blood feuds extended from generation to generation. When the country was steeped into utter darkness, the light of Islam dawned and it illuminated the whole world. The Prophet Muhammad (peace and blessings of Allah be upon him) appeared as a warner and harbinger of glad tiding. He summoned the depraved community to the right path in the teeth of bitter opposition. While his distinguished Companions stood by him through thick and thin. They shared his sufferings and stood firm like a rock buffeting the waves of hostility with such a strong conviction as had no parallel in the annals of history. After a great deal of endeavour by the Holy Prophet (peace and blessings of Allah be upon him) with his illustrious Companions like Hadrat Abu Bakr, 'Umar, 'Uthman and 'Ali (may Allah be pleased with them) many social evils were swept out. The hostile tribes were united in faith and obedience. They were all joined into brotherhood cemented with amity and concord. Their fighting spirit was tamed and their quarrels were appeased and forgotton. The wild untutored sons of the desert, spoilt children of the obscure land, veilded in mystery and darkness, were pulled out into light, brilliance and dazzling. The Holy Prophet (peace and blessings of Allah be upon him) was just like the moon, whereas Hadrat Abu Bakr, 'Umar, 'Uthman and 'Ali (may Allah be pleased with them) bore resemblance to the beams of the moon. They were all of equal status. They had sound friendly relations with one another. It is undesirable to make any distinction in them. Whosoever finds fault with any one of them may invoke the wrath of Allah. He should feel penitent of this act of impudence. Some of the historians have tried to deface the fair image of Hadrat 'Uthman, in spite of the fact that he occupies a prominent position among the Companions due to his attachment to his Master (peace and blessings of Allah be upon him) and the glorious services rendered by him to the cause of Islam. His noble soul faced martyrdom, but he avoided becoming the root cause of dissensions in the Muslim Community. He refrained from using force till the last moments of his life.

The main purpose of writing this book is to acquaint the readers with the real situation. The allegations levelled against Hadrat 'Uthman were absolutely baseless. His character was perfectly free of the blemish imputed to him out of malice just for the sake of false propaganda.

I am deeply indebted to the veteran scholar Prof. 'Abdul Hameed Siddiqi who has been kind enough to revise the manuscript of this book and make valuable suggestions.

I am also grateful to Mr. M. A. Qazi of the Kazi Publications who has undertaken to publish this book with the fervour of a religious devotee.

My younger brothers Messers Muhammad Iqbal Shaikh and Muhammad Ikram and my friend Karamat 'Ali also deserve my special thanks for their help and assistance.

'ABDUR RAHMAN SHAD

allegations levelled against Hazrat Uthman were absolutely baseless. His character was perfectly free of the faults imputed to him out of malice and for the sake of false propaganda.

I am deeply indebted to Prof. Abdul Hameed Siddiqui who has been kind enough to revise the manuscript of this book and make valuable suggestions.

I am also grateful to Mr. M. S. Qazi of the Kazi Publications who has undertaken to publish this book with the fervour of a religious devotee.

My younger brothers Messrs Muhammad Iqbal Shah and Muhammad Ikram and my friend Rahmat Ali also deserve my special thanks for their help and assistance.

ABDUL RAHMAN SHAD

'UTHMAN BIN 'AFFAN

(may Allah be pleased with him)

EARLY LIFE

Hadhrat 'Uthmān was the third Caliph of Islam. Before the acceptance of Islam, he was known by his patronym Abu 'Amr. His father's name was 'Affan and the name of his mother was Arwa. His grandmother Baida' was the daughter of 'Abdul Muttalib and, therefore, she was an aunt of the Prophet (peace and blessings of Allah be upon him). His lineage joins that of the Prophet (peace and blessings of Allah be upon him). He belonged to the Banu Umayya, tribe of the Quraish. This tribe enjoyed a position of distinction because its people were entrusted with the custody of the national flag of this community. It was an office of rare honour and dignity. He was born six years after the birth of the Prophet (peace and blessings of Allah be upon him). He was honest, modest and upright even as a child. When he was young, he adopted trade as his profession and earned wealth in abundance. Thus he was awarded the title of *'Ghani'* Before the advent of Islam the darkness of ignorance prevailed everywhere in Arabia.

Only a few men could read and write. 'Uthmān was one of those fortunate souls who were literate. Even before embracing Islam, he commanded great respect for his integrity, piety, humility and kind-heartedness. He abstained from drinking and gambling. He had an extremely affectionate nature. He never oppressed his fellow beings. He never deceived anyone because he was fair in all his dealings. All spoke highly of him due to his polite habits and polished manners. He was generous at heart and missed no chance to remove the sufferings of those less fortunate than himself. He won a lot of admiration due to his noble qualities of head and heart.

ACCEPTANCE OF ISLAM

Abu Bakr and 'Uthmān (may Allah be pleased with them) were fast friends. Abu Bakr explained to his friend 'Uthmān the sublime teachings of Islam. Gradually he tried to persuade him to embrace Islam. He convinced 'Uthmān that the Prophet (peace and blessings of Allah *be* upon him) was a truthful man, his religion was true and he was the Messenger of Allah. One day 'Uthmān and Talhs were returning from Syria when they had a novel experience. On the way they sat down to take rest. Being extremely tired they were feeling drowsy. A vision appeared before them saying,

"Arise, you sleeping ones, Ahmad has appeared in Makkah". After this they proceeded to the Prophet (peace and blessings of Allah be upon him) and affirmed their faith *in* Allah and His Messenger. Although leading men of the Banu Umayya such as Abu Sufyan and Mu'ait were the sworn enemies of the Prophet (peace and blessings of Allah be upon him), yet 'Uthmān was not influenced by this rivalry. When Truth dawned on him, he embraced Islam without hesitation and not caring for the dire consequences.

UTHMAN SUBJECTED TO TORTURE

The infidels made the Muslims the victim of intolerable torture but they could not banish Islam from their hearts. Even 'Uthman who was held in high esteem by the Quraish, underwent a lot of inconvenience. When his uncle Hakam heard of his conversion, he tied his hands and feet with a rope and threw him in a dark dungeon. He was warned that he would never be set free until he had renounced the new faith. 'Uthmān (may Allah be pleased with him) faced all sorts of hardships in following the path of Islam with unshakable determination and a smiling countenance. He replied that he believed in Allah and His Prophet (peace and blessings of Allah be upon him). He would never forsake Islam, come what may. At last Hakam, his uncle, had to yield. He could not detain him indefinitely in the dungeon and so he had no alternative but to release him.

MIGRATION TO ABYSSINIA AND MEDINAH

When the persecution of the Muslims exceeded all bounds, the Prophet (peace and blessings of Allah be upon him) advised them to emigrate to Abyssinia. The ruler of that kingdom, the Negus was Christian by religion. He was a kind-hearted and pious man. He gave shelter to the oppressed Muslims. Under the directions of the Master (peace and blessings of Allah be upon him), 'Uthmān left his kith and kin and other possessions for the sake of Allah and went to Abyssinia. Ruqayya, his wife and daughter of the Prophet (peace and blessings of Allah be upon him) accompanied him. They lived there for a few years and returned to Makkah again when a rumour was afloat that all the pagans of Makkah had entered in the fold of Islam. Indeed this false and fabricated news was circulated to dupe the Muslims. The disbelievers had played a trick to call the innocent Muslims back and make them the victims of their tortures again. The infidels, however, succeeded in their mission. Most of the Muslims returned to their Holy City and the infidels had another opportunity to persecute them. The converts bore all sorts of hardships with steadfastness. Allah gave glad tidings to such persons in the Holy Qur'an:

> "And those who flee for Allah's sake after they are oppressed, We will most certainly give them a good abode in the world....."
>
> *(An-Nahal : 41)*

When the fourteenth year of the Call to Prophethood began, Allah commanded the believers to migrate to Madinah. 'Uthmān and his wife Ruqayya emigrated with the rest of the companions and settled there. The emigrant Muslims of Makkah strengthened the ties of friendship and brotherhood with the inhabitants of Madinah in the light of the following verse of the Holy Qur'an :

> "Surely those who believed and fled (from their homes) and struggled hard in the path of Allah with their property and their souls and those who gave shelter and helped—these are the guardians of each other...."
>
> *(Al-Infi'al : 72)*

The Helpers embraced their brethren-in-faith with sacrificial spirit and the new-comers did not take undue advantage of their sympathy. They tried to put a minimum burden on them. As 'Uthmān was a well-to-do merchant, he helped the needy and the poor in both the sects. So they expressed their gratitude to him for shouldering some responsibilities on their behalf.

VALUABLE SERVICES TO ISLAM

After emigrating to Madinah 'Uthmān (may Allah be pleased with him) rendered meritorious services to the cause of Islam. When the Muslim refugees came to Madinah, there was an acute dearth of water. There was only one well to meet the requirements of the residents of that locality. It was owned by the Jews. They did not allow the Muslims to draw water from the well. They charged a heavy price for it from the Muslims. 'Uthmān purchased that well for twenty thousand Dirhams and placed it at the disposal of the Muslims. When the Prophet's Mosque appeared too small to accommodate the rapidly increasing number of beli-evers, 'Uthmān (may Allah be pleased with him) bought the adjoining piece of land and added it to the Mosque for extension. 'Uthmān was one of the scribes of the Master (peace and blessings of Allah be upon him). He wrote down portions of the Holy Qur'an as they were revealed.

'Uthmān participated in various holy battles against the infidels. He took an active part in the battle of Uhud. He also participated in the battles of Khaibar and Hunain and performed many heroic deeds to glorify

Islam. On the occasion of the Treaty of Hudaibiya, the Prophet (peace and blessings of Allah be upon him) desired to send 'Umar (may Allah be pleased with him) with the message to the Makkans but he made the following reply :

> "O Prophet ! The Quraish are well aware of my feelings towards them as are manifest by many inimical acts of mine. They will not like to hold discussions with me in connection with the terms of a peaceful settlement. I can point out a man whose influence will be much more efficacious than mine. I mean 'Uthman ibn 'Affan".

The Prophet (peace and blessings of Allah be upon him) recognizing this to be sound counsel, despatched 'Uthmān to Abu Sufyan and the other leaders of the Quraish. 'Uthmān carried, out the orders of his Master (peace and blessings of Allah be upon him) without hesitation and reached Makkah, The first man whom 'Uthmān met was Abad bin Sa'id. He put himself under his protection during the course of the negotiation. When the Prophet's envoy had finished explaining the aim and object of his mission to the prominent men of Makkah, they said, "0 'Uthmān ! If you are desirous of performing the ritual circuits *(Tawaf),* you are allowed to do so but we have sworn not to permit entry to Muhammad (peace and blessings of Allah be upon him). At once 'Uthmān replied, "I will never accomplish them unless I am following the footsteps of Allah's Messenger (peace and blessings of Allah be upon him). It is unthinkable that I take preference over the Master (peace and blessings of Allah be upon him)". This answer exasperated the Quraish. They behaved arrogantly with him. They imprisoned him despite his rank of ambassador. In the meantime the rumour spread that 'Uthmān had been murdered in cold blood by the enemies of Allah. There was a stir *in* the Muslim Camp and the believers were overwhelmed with Utmost indignation. The Prophet (peace and blessings of Allah be upon him) also thought that 'Uthmān had been murdered as there was no news to the contrary. If so, the Quraish had been guilty of the most heinous sin of the murder of an Arab Chief in the sacred month inside the sacred territory. The Prophet (peace and blessings of Allah be upon him) hesitated no longer and proclaimed :

> "We will not go back until we have taken revenge of the murder of 'Uthman and punished the infidels for this abominable crime".

'Umar (may Allah be pleased with him) acting under the orders of the Prophet (peace and blessings of Allah be upon him) announced at the top of his voice:

> "O Believers ! Come and take a fresh pledge of allegiance to avenge the murder of 'Uthman".

The Prophet (peace and blessings of Allah be upon him) sitting under the shade of a gum tree, awaited the Faithful who came hastening to him. They quivered with enthusiasm and resolved to follow him faithfully. Fourteen hundred Muslims made the pledge to the Prophet (peace and blessings of Allah be upon him) and determined to fight undauntedly to take vengeance for the blood of 'Uthmān. As 'Uthmān was not present at that time, the Prophet (peace and blessings of Allah be upon him) placed one of his hands on the other and said that this was a pledge from 'Uthman. This shows the esteem in which the Prophet (peace and blessings of Allah be upon him) held 'Uthman. This pledge is called the Bai'at ar-Ridwan, because Allah was pleased with it. A reference regarding this event has been made in the Holy Qur'an :

> "Surely Allah was pleased with the believers when they swore allegiance to thee under the tree. He knew what was in their hearts, therefore He sent down tranquillity upon them and rewarded them with ensuing; victory. And with large prizes of war which, they took; for Allah is Mighty, Wise"
>
> (*Al-Fatah : 18, 19*)

The Bai'at ar-Ridwan manifested intense agitation. It was an act of dauntless self-sacrifice for the cause of Truth and, as such a red-letter event in the annals of Islam. History affords no better example of

"All for one and one for all". The Quraish were so impressed by the sight of this display of devotion that they set 'Uthman (may Allah be pleased with him) at liberty and sent Suhail bin 'Amr with a flag of truce. After a good deal of deliberations the Treaty of Hudaibiya was signed.

In the year 9 A. H., reports reached the Prophet (peace and blessings of Allah be upon, him) that the mighty Emperor of Byzantine was preparing to march on Madinah. These reports disturbed the Muslims. The Prophet (peace and blessings of Allah be upon him) began to make counter-preparations. He called upon the Muslims to help him in this hour of need. In response to the appeal of the Prophet (peace and blessings of Allah be upon him), before the expedition of Tabuk, 'Uthman contributed ten thousand Dinars in cash and one thousand camels along with fifty horses. He bore the expenses of a major part of the army.

'UTHMAN'S ROLE BEFORE THE ERA OF HIS CALIPHATE

'Uthman was the true devotee and follower of the Prophet (peace and blessings of Allah be upon him). He stood by him through thick and thin throughout his life. He helped his Master (peace and blessings of Allah be upon him) at every critical juncture. He accompanied him during the Farewell Pilgrimage and looked after him when he was on his death-bed. After the demise of his beloved Master (peace and blessings of Allah be upon him) he rendered whole-hearted assistance to his successors, Abu Bakr and 'Umar (may Allah be pleased with them). He was a prominent figure in the Council of Advisers *(Majlis-e-Shura)* and he was consulted in every matter. His counsels were highly praised, and appreciated. Every duty which was assigned to him, was performed by him honestly, efficiently and diligently. When the time for Abu Bakr to depart this earthly life drew near, he was anxious to nominate a suitable person to succeed him. He sought the advice of 'Abdur Rahman bin 'Auf and 'Uthman in this connection. The same position of confidence was enjoyed by him during the Caliphate of 'Umar (may Allah be pleased with him).

'UTHMAN'S ELECTION AS CALIPH

After the sad demise of the Prophet (peace and blessings of Allah be upon him) Abu Bakr was elected as the first Caliph of the prophet. He commanded universal respect due to his piety, integrity, honesty and close association with his Master (peace and blessings of Allah be upon. him). He had gained a good deal of administrative experience. All eyes, therefore, spontaneously turned to him and he was asked to shoulder the responsibilities as the Head of the Islamic State. Likewise, after the death of Abu Bakr, 'Umar (may Allah be pleased with them) was unanimously elected as the second Caliph of Islam because he was a man of conspicuous calibre. He was a person with rare attainments and versatile gifts. He was a daring soldier and a successful ruler. After these towering personalities, there were some other illustrious companions of the Prophet '(peace and blessings of Allah be upon him) but the question of a choice out of so many persons, fit for the exalted office, was a matter of some anxiety. 'Umar (may Allah be pleased with him) himself nominated none as the third Caliph but constituted a board of the following six Electors to choose his successor :

1. 'Uthman bin 'Affan
2. 'Ali ibn Abi Talib.
3. 'Abdur Rahman bin 'Auf
4. Sa'd bin Abi Waqqas
5. Talha bin 'Ubaidullah
6. Zubair bin 'Awwam

After the constitution of the Board of Electors,

'Umar gave instructions to the members concerned to finish their task within three days after his death. He fully realized that secrecy and speed in electing his successor were imperative lest the impatient people resort to trouble and thereby imperil the unity and stability of the Islamic State. .

Soon after the death of 'Umar the meeting of the Electors was convened and the issue of his successor was discussed. Zubair withdrew his name in favour of 'Ali and Talha withdrew to support 'Uthman. He declared that 'Uthman was a more deserving candidate than himself to mannge the affairs of the Islamic State. Sa'd bin Abi Waqqas declined to shoulder the responsibilities of the Caliphate and proposed the name of 'Abdur Rahman bin 'Auf for this exalted office. At last, out of six, only two candidates 'Uthman and 'Ali were left in the field. It was decided that 'Abdur Rahman bin 'Auf should act as an Umpire in order to solve this knotty problem. All agreed to abide by his decision. 'Abdur Rahman bin 'Auf consulted the prominent figures of the nation on this burning issue. The consensus of opinion was in favour of 'Uthman. On the fourth day after the morning prayer many people had assembled in the Mosque. 'Abdur Rahman bin 'Auf called 'Uthman and said, "Promise that, you shall act according to the commandments of the Holy Qur'an and the noble examples set by the Prophet (peace and blessings of Allah be upon him) and his two Caliphs." 'Uthman solemnly promised to do so to the best of his knowledge and ability. So 'Abdur Rahman bin 'Auf declared him as the duly elected Caliph. He pledged loyalty to him. His example was followed by 'Ali, Talha, Zubair, Sa'd bin Abi Waqqas and many others. The people followed them with promptitude and took the oath of allegiance at the hands of the newly elected Caliph.

FIRST ADDRESS AS A CALIPH

When the pledge of fidelity was over,. 'Uthman rose to address the gathering. His feeble body was quivering under the burden of the new responsibilities of Caliphate. He said :

> "We are dwellers of the place of retribution. Our lives are mortal and short-lived. We should try our best to do noble acts as far as possible because we have to become a victim of death. Everyone of us will be answerable to our Lord on the Day of Judgement. Remember, life lacks in reliability and death keeps no calendar. This world is full of illusions. Take a warning from those who were voluptuous. They enjoyed all comforts of life in the world but returned to dust with ignominy. Verily, Allah is the Beneficent and does not take prompt action against the sinners. He provides us the

opportunities to reform ourselves. We should not take undue advantage of His affability. We should, therefore, become God-conscious. We should not invoke His Wrath by doing evil deeds, We should try to win the favours of Allah by performing noble acts which shall reward us in the Eternal Abode."

(Ibn Kathlr, *Al-Bidaya wal-Nihaya)*

FIRST DECISION AS A JUDGE

The first case that came for hearing before Caliph 'Uthman was very complicated. It was against 'Ubaidullah, the son of 'Umar. He had murdered two Persians named Hurmuzan and Jafna. He did so because he suspected that they were the connivers of Abu Lu'lu', the murderer of his beloved father. The evening before 'Umar was stabbed, 'Abdur Rahman had seen them standing with Abu Lu'lu' and whispering in a doubtful manner. When he approached them, they were perplexed and a double-edged sharp dagger fell down on the ground. After the martyrdom of 'Umar the dagger was carefully examined and recognised to be the same because it coincided exactly with the description given by 'Abdur Rahman bin Abi Bakr. On the basis of this evidence, 'Ubaidullah felt sure that Abu Lu'lu' alone was not responsible for killing his father but Hurmuzan and Jafna were also involved in this conspiracy. He flew into a rage and put them to sword. 'Uthman consulted some distinguished companions in connection with this complicated case. 'Ali expressed his opinion that the evidence of one man was not sufficient to hold Hurmuzan and Jafna guilty. So he proposed the death sentence for 'Ubaidullah. The other companions, however, did not concur with this opinion. 'Uthman was in vacillation. At last he found a way out of the difficulty. He himself paid the ransom for the two victims and acquitted 'Ubaidullah. As they had no relatives, the Caliph had a lawful right to act on their behalf. This sagacious decision of the Caliph was appreciated by all.

FIRST DIRECTIVE AS CALIPH

Caliph 'Uthman (may Allah be pleased with him) issued a directive to all Governors, Revenue Collectors and Military Officers. They were advised to be just in their dealings, honest in pecuniary matters and tolerant towards the non-Muslims. They should not feel ostentatious of their high posts. They were the humblest servants of the people. They should serve them whole-heartedly. They were not their rulers and masters. They were the guardians of the people. It was their moral duty to maintain peace and order to give a sense of security to civil life.

CONQUESTS

The caliphate of 'Uthman especially its first few years, added another splendid chapter to the annals of Islam. The momentum of Muslim victories continued in all directions during the period of his caliphate.

Revolt in Persia

The mutineers in Persia rose in open insurrection against the authority of Islam. The ex-King Yazdejird was the root cause of this mischief. He incited the public to revolt against the new Caliph who sacked Abu Musa Ash'ari from the post of Governor and appointed 'Abdullah bin 'Amir instead of him. 'Uthman despatched troops to the scene and controlled the situation with an iron hand. Although 'Abdullah bin 'Amir was a young man, yet he proved himself to be an intrepid General. He marched against the Persian rebels in Southern and Central Persia and suppressed the rebellion in no time. He despatched his lieutenants towards the provinces situated in the remote east for further conquests. He extended his operations to the frontiers from where the whole trouble had originated. Then he advanced upon Khurasan where Yazdejird still lurked. He captured its capital, Nishapur. The ex-King fled towards Merv which was also conquered in the year 30 A. H. Then Yazdejird ran towards Tur near the

Oxus to seek the help of the Turks. In 32 A.H., the Muslim army had an encounter with the Turkish forces in the valley of Azarbaijan. At first the Muslims were forced to retreat but on the arrival of reinforcements, they put their opponents to rout. 'Abdullah bin 'Amir conquered Khawarizm as well and retrieved the good reputation of the soldiers of Allah. After these splendid victories he returned to Basra with 40,000 captives and visited Makkah to perform 'Umra, the lesser pilgrimage, for thanksgiving.

Although Yazdejird had lost his empire he had not lost hope. He wandered from place to place and created unrest and confusion. He tried to seek help from the rulers of the Far East but to no avail. His last exploit was a raid on Sajistan. With the assistance of the chiefs of Turkistan, he invaded Sajistan but was completely defeated. He ran away for his iife. He took shelter in a watermill. The diamonds and jewels of the ex-King incited the avarice of the miller who killed him to take possession of his riches. He threw his dead body in the river. Thus the last Emperor of Persia died and the constant trouble came to an end.

The Conquest of Armenia

Caliph 'Uthman deputed Salman bin Rabia and Habib bin Muslima to re-conquer Armenia. In the campaign Habib's wife also accompanied him. She was a

daggers and swords took place. The forces of the enemy were unable to withstand the furious onslaught of the Muslims and were routed. Many of the ships were either burnt to ashes or sunk, to the depths of the sea. The remainder fled to Syracuse in Sicily.

The Arab victory at Alexandria was splendid and momentous. It shattered the naval supremacy of the Byzantine empire in the Eastern Mediterranean. It removed the constant danger of the enemy incursions into Egypt and Syria, and established a good reputation of the Arab navy.

CAUSES OF UNPOPULARITY

During the first six years of the Caliphate of 'Uthman (may Allah be pleased with him) perfect allevation and peace reigned everywhere. The people enjoyed all sorts of comforts. The frontiers were extended and fortified and many new territories were added to the Empire. The soldiers of Allah had performed numerous heroic deeds in naval warfare. The country made a remarkable progress in trade and agriculture. Emissaries to preach Islam went far and wide and thousands of people entered the fold of Islam. Some new converts were not yet fascinated by the charm of Islam. Their convictions were not firm. They had wavering minds. Apparently, they professed to be Muslims but they were not sincere at heart. Such people were hypocrites and they did not lose any opportunity to deface the image of Islam. They incited the simple-minded and guileless converts to rebel against the Muslim authority. They tried to disrupt the administrative machinery of the Government. They fabricated false stories to create dissatisfaction and unrest in the country. Their sole aim was to undermine Islam under the garb of Islam. Gradually their efforts bore fruit and some of the new converts lost respect for their new faith.

Bedouins' Jealousy

'Umar (may Allah be pleassed with him) had imposed restrictions on the Arab settlers in the provinces against acquiring lands. He had also banned the migration of the Quraish to the newly conquered provinces but 'Uthman (may Allah be pleased with him) gradually abolished all these salutary restraints. He allowed the Quraish to acquire agricultural properties in the provinces and also to settle there. Above all, he allotted lands and estates to the Arabs. Thus the Quraish were enriched by the immense spoils of wars and by the new estates they had received. They began to lead a life full of luxury and enjoyment. Moreover, most of the Quraish were exempted from the payment of tribute. The Bedouins were aggrieved because the lands which they had conquered with their swords, were allotted to those new settlers who had done nothing for their subjugation. The mischief mongers took advantage of this situation and incited the proud Bedouins. They added fuel to the fire and started the propaganda against the third Caliph of Islam. They dinned into the ears of the tribes that they were being deprived of their basic due rights. The Quraish were provided with all the facilities of life and all the profitable offices were monopolized by them. This propaganda had a vicious effect on the-minds of the Bedouins. Their grievances, therefore, turned into resentment against the policy of 'Uthman. This dissatisfaction found its eloquent expression in the new cities of Basra, Kufa and Fustat. The unruly and factious spirit of the inhabitants of these cities had already created disorder during the Caliphate of 'Umar (may Allah be pleased with him) who had to change Governors in Basra and Kufa frequently. As 'Uthman (may Allah be pleased with him) was a kind-hearted and vacil lating successor, the Bedouins of these areas became seditious during his reign.

Abuse of the Spirit of Democracy by Miscreants

Islam stands for perfect equality of man irrespective of earthly distinctions. It never imposed restrictions on freedom of thought and expression. During the Caliphate of Abu Bakr, Umar and 'Uthman (may Allah be pleased with them) the position of the Head of the Islamic State was not higher than that of a common man. He was open to criticism. Anybody could find fault with him. The Governors were made accessible to the public. They were forbidden to have servants to serve them and personal guards to look after them. They were dismissed if the geniune complaint was lodged against them. They were at the mercy of the public. This unlimited freedom was a deadly weapon in the hands of mischievous persons who frequently tried to upset the administrative machinery of the Government.

Internal Differences of the Quraish

Uthman would have suppressed the disruptionists, had he secured the full support of the Quraish. The Quraish were split up into three factions. Banu Umayya were led by 'Uthman and 'Ali was the Chief of Banu Hashim. The orthodox sect consisted of the surviving companions and their descendants. 'Uthman's clemency for his relatives provoked indignation and criticism of the rival factions of the Quraish and of the other tribes. Consequently, a number of the most important offices went into the hands of the Umayyads. This offended Banu Hashim and their supporters. Moreover, 'Uthman allowed his uncle Hakam bin 'As and his kinsmen to reside in Madinah. The Prophet (peace and blessings of Allah be upon him) had expelled him from Madinah. Before the advent of Islam, he was his neighbour and he used to tease him every now and then. This was the man who persecuted 'Uthman when the latter embraced Islam. Although he had embraced Islam he was still not sincere at heart. His attitude towards Islam was buffoonery. One of his kinsmen Marwan had occupied a prominent position in the Caliphate of 'Uthman. He was a clever man and was looked down upon by the Alides. "The atmosphere of bitter opposition to authority prevailed when the Caliph dismissed various Governors who were the leading companions of the Prophet (peace and blessings of Allah be upon him). They were towering personalities like Abu Musa Ash'ari, Mughira bin Shu'ba, 'Amr bin al-'As and Sa'd bin Abi Waqqas. They joined the ranks of the critics of the Caliph. Their opposition had a deep effect on the Muslims because they had rendered meritorious services to the cause of Islam.

CHANGES OF GOVERNORS

Kufa : 'Umar had appointed Mughira bin Shu'ba as the Governor of Kufa. He was sacked by 'Uthman on his accession. He appointed Sa'd bin Abi Waqqas according to the instructions of his predecessor. Now there arose a dispute between Sa'd, the Governor and

Ibn Mas'ud, the Treasury Officer of Kufa. Sa'd had taken a loan from the Treasury and had not paid it back in time due to unavoidable circumstances. When Ibn Mas'ud reminded the Governor to pay the debt, there ensued some altercation which developed into an open dispute. As such, this state of affairs was against the interests of the solidarity of the community, the Caliph replaced Sa'd by Walid bin 'Aqba. He was a strong man. He took drastic action, against the defaulters. One night some mischief-mongers broke into the house of a man. They took away all his possessions and murdered him in cold blood. They were arrested and put to death. The death of this gang made the Sabaites angry. A strong man like Walid was a danger to them. They started malicious propaganda against him. They said that Walid was a close relative of the Caliph. His father was a rabid opponent of Islam, he participated in the battle of Badr, was captured and put to the sword by the orders of the Prophet (peace and blessings of Allah be upon him). Above all, he was accused of drinking wine. One day, they lodged a false complaint against him and demanded his dismissal. Walid was not only sacked but physically awarded the prescribed number of stripes according to the law of Islam. After the dismissal of Walid bin 'Aqba, the Caliph appointed in his place Sa'id bin al-'As who was also a kinsman of the Caliph. Although he was an enterprising warrior he was an inexperienced administrator. The new Governor gave a reception to the people at his house at night. He discussed various matters with them. The Sabaites attended these meetings in large numbers. They began to act according to their own wishes. Gradually they started creating trouble. Things became so intolerable that some people requested the Caliph to rid the city of these hooligans. Consequently, he was replaced by Abu Musa Ash'ari who was not a blood relative of the Caliph. The Caliph left no stone unturned to satisfy the disruptionists but their nature could not be changed.

Egypt : 'Amr bin al-'As was the Governor of Egypt when 'Uthman became the Caliph. 'Uthman dismissed him and appointed 'Abdullah bin Sarah in his place. He was no doubt a capable administrator. He increased the revenues of Egypt. He defeated a powerful Byzantine army near Carthage. He was the first Admiral of Islam who inflicted a decisive naval defeat on the Byzantine Navy near Alexandria. Unfortunately, he was the foster brother of the Caliph. In spite of all his good qualities of head and heart, 'Abdullah had a blot on his fair name. He had the bad reputation of a renegade. He embraced Islam before the conquest of Makkah. He was employed by the Prophet (peace and blessings of Allah be upon him) to write down Revelations. Once he tampered with what he wrote. The Prophet (peace and blessings of Allah be upon him) came to know of this mischief and heresy.

'Abdullah fled to Makkah where he apostatised. After the fall of Makkah, he was arrested. He was sentenced to death as a renegade. But he was forgiven by the Prophet (peace and blessings of Allah be upon him), on the intercession of "Uthman. The mischief-mongers raked up the past events and blamed the Caliph for showing favours to his kith and kin. 'Ali suggested the Caliph to dismiss 'Abdullah bin Abi Sarah and appoint Muhammad bin Abu Bakr instead. 'Uthman acted upon his suggestion without hesitation.

Basra : The situation also deteriorated in Basra. Abu Musa Ash'ari, the Governor of Basra was replaced by 'Abdullah bin 'Amir. He was the cousin of the Caliph. He was an intrepid General. He crushed the revolt in Persia and extended the frontier of the Empire by launching successful campaigns in the East. He was accused of filling all key-posts with his relatives. The people of Basra raised a storm of opposition against him. 'Abdullah bin 'Amir was a talented young man. He was deeply religious.

He acted according to the desires of the public. He established a brilliant record of victories. Once he wrapped himself in white sheets *(Ihram)* inside his province and set out to perform an off-seasonal pilgrimage ('Umrah) to Makkah to express a deep sense of gratitude to Almighty Allah. It was an act of exaggera-tion in religion. When 'Uthman came to know of this, he reprimanded him. But the mischief-mongers found another opportunity to add to the unpopularity of the innocent Caliph. He was held responsible even for the faults of his officers.

Deportation Of Abu Dharr

A remarkable change had occurred in the Arabs. The victories and spoils of war had made them the owners of immense riches. They began to lead luxurious lives. Some devout Muslims considered this way of living as un Islamic and against the simple and abstemious teachings of Islam and practice of the Prophet (peace and blessings of Allah be upon him). One of them was Abu Dharr, a close associate of the Prophet (peace and blessing of Allah bo upon him). He was a man of retiring temperament. He was one of the early converts and vehemently denounced riches. During his visit to Damascus, he was nearly shocked to see the fashionable living of the Muslims under the Governorship of Mu'awiya. He expressed his sentiments in many speeches. He warned the Muslims of the torment of Hell for the pomp and vanities. He argued that wealth was to be spent on charitable objects only and it should not be hoarded. He quoted the following verse of the Holy Qur'an in support of his views :

> "Those who hoard up gold and silver and spend it not in the way of Allah, tell them of a painful doom on the day when it will be heated in the fire of hell. Then their foreheads, their flanks and their backs shall be branded therewith. Here is what you hoarded for yourselves. Now taste of what you used to hoard."
>
> (*At-Tawbah : 34*)

Abu Dharr's views made a great appeal to the masses. As the majority of the people were poor, they desired to share the comforts of the rich. This movement began to gain ground rapidly. It created a stir in the society. Consequently, Mu'awiya sent Abu Dharr to Madinah where the Caliph argued with him. He said :

> "O Abu Dharr ! I will force people to pay whatever they owe to Allah and His Apostle (peace and blessings of Allah be upon him). In return, I will grant them the rights, they have over me. But I can force none to part with his wealth."

Abu Dharr was not satisfied. He insisted on preaching his views. He denounced riches as ungodly. He refused to live among such people and requested the Caliph to allow him to go somewhere else. He was sent to Rabadha, situated at a distance of about twenty miles from Madinah. 'Ammar bin Yasir and 'Ali were the supporters of Abu Dharr. They criticised the Caliph for this treatment but Abu Dharr said :

> "If Uthman hangs me from the tallest branch of the palm-tree, I will never disobey him."

These words were a clear manifestation of his staunch obedience to the Caliph (Ameer) in spite of the bitter difference of opinions. After two years Abu Dharr died in self-adorned distress and penury. His death too had been a burning topic of the day. The disruptionists unhesitatingly blamed the Caliph for meting out cruel treatment to such a saintly man.

Enlargement of the Courtyard of the Ka'bah

Another pious act of the noble Caliph badly affected his reputation. It was the enlargement of the courtyard around the Ka'bah in 647 A.D. The owners, whose houses were demolished for the purpose, raised a great hue and cry against the Caliph notwithstanding the fact that they were handsomely compensated. They also joined the detractors and critics of the Caliph.

The Matter of Shortened Prayers

It was the practice to perform shortened Prayers at the time of the pilgrimage. On one occasion, 'Uthman offered full prayers contrary to the practice of the Prophet (peace and blessings of Allah be upon him) and the first two Caliphs. This change in the ceremony of the Hajj victimized the Caliph to the charge of innovation in the matter of religion.

Standardisation of the Holy Qur'an

During the Caliphate of 'Uthman (may Allah be pleased with him) controversy began over the correct recitation of the Holy Quran. The Arabs of 'Iraq claimed that their recitation was more accurate. They followed 'Abdullah bin Mas'ud in this respect. The Syrians followed Miqdad bin Aswad and insisted that their recitation was more authentic. When the Caliph was informed of this controversy, he consulted his advisers and the illustrious companions of the Prophet (peace and blessings of Allah be upon him). It was decided that an authentic text based on the copy in Hadhrat Hafsa's (Allah be plased with her) custody be issued as the standard text. Accordingly, copies of the original text were prepared and despatched to the provincial headquarters to serve as standard text and reference edition. Some of the scripts were burnt to prevent any future controversy. The original text was preserved during the Caliphate of Abu Bakr as described by Ibn Kathir in *al-Bidaya wal-Nihdya.*

"During the reign of Abu Bakr, a large number of distinguished Qur'an conners (Hafiz) were martyred in the battle of Yamama. 'Umar suggested the Caliph to have authentic copies of the original text made to preserve it. Abu Bakr ordered Zaid bin Thabit to write down the true copy of the Holy Qur'an revealed to the Prophet (peace and blessings of Allah be upon him). He did so in compliance with the orders of the Caliph. This authentic text remained in the custody of Abu Bakr and 'Umar (may Allah be pleased with them). 'Uthman obtained it from the daughter of the second Caliph, Hafsa. He ordered Zaid bin Thabit and Sa'id bin al-'As to prepare its true copies for circulation. This work was carried out under the supervision of 'Abdullah bin Zubair and 'Abdur Rahman bin Harith. 'Abdullah bin Mas'ud refused to accept this standard text and claimed his own as the authentic one. The factious people of Kufa accused the Caliph of burning and tampering with the Holy Qur'an. The mischief-mongers started propaganda that an act of great sacrilege had been committed. A great hue and cry was raised and the agitators incited the ignorant Muslims against the Caliph. On this occasion 'Ali declared :

"O People ! Do not show waywardness in respect of 'Uthman. You accuse him of burning the Holy

Qur'an. By God, he had done so with the consultation of the companions of the Prophet. Had I been Caliph instead of him, I would have acted in the same manner." *(Tabaqat ibn Sa'd)*

Besides, Abu Huraira congratulated 'Uthman on the accomplishment of this commendable task.

(Bukhari)

It was a laudable act of faith on the part of the Caliph who preserved the correctness and purity of the Holy Qur'an. For this act, posterity is highly grateful to 'Uthman. In the record of his services for the cause of Islam, this particular one must stand on the top. 'Uthman was not the Collector of the Holy Qur'an, as was generally thought, but he provided the world of Islam with a single uniform edition of the Holy Qur'an. In this way the Last Book of Allah remained immune from all sorts of additions and alterations.

'ABDULLAH BIN SABA LEADS AGITATION

The time was now ripe for the disruptionists to incite the discontented people against the Caliph. The Arab tribes were disgusted with the pretensions of the Quraish while the Quraish of the Banu Hashim were dissatisfied with the behaviour of the Umayyads. In such a conflicting atmosphere appeared a cunning man named 'Abdullah bin Saba with the surname Ibn Sa'uda. He was a Jew of the Yemen. He played a villain's role in this drama. During the Caliphate of 'Uthman, he migrated to Basra and accepted Islam with an ulterior motive to wreck its unity and subvert its theology. He preached a new version of Islam known as Sabaism. He put forth the following convictions :

> "The Prophet has not died. He has only disappeared. He will re-appear just like the Christ. Every Prophet left behind a Wasi. The Wasi must be a near relative of the Prophet. Jush bin Nun was the Wasi of Moses. Similarly, the Prophet must also have a Wasi to carry on his mission. Muhammad (peace and blessings of Allah be upon him) was the Last Prophet. So his Wasi, 'Ali was the last of the Wasis. Being the Wasi, 'Ali was the only rightful man to become the Caliph. 'Uthman, therefore, had deprived 'Ali of his right."
>
> (Ibn Kathir, *Al-Bidaya wal-Nihaya)*

'Abdullah feigned himself a devout Muslim. He was bent upon causing dissension among the believers in order to arrest the onward march of Islam. He hatched different plots to achieve his evil designs. When he succeeded in injecting, the venom of hatred in some people, he organised a party in Basra consisting of those men who were discontented with the Governor 'Abdullah bin 'Amir. But the Governor expelled him from the city. Then he came to Kufa but the Governor concerned turned him out. Then he proceeded to Syria where he failed to find a fertile land suitable for the-growth of the sapling of friction and hatred. This province was protected from 'Abdullah bin Saba's ominous influence by the prudence of Mu'awiya who did not allow these wicked people to stay in Syria. Finally, he chose Egypt to be the headquarters of his party. Egypt lay in the eastern and western wings of the empire. Its Governor 'Abdullah bin Sarrah was an inexperienced administrator. He was appointed in place of 'Amr bin al-'As who was a popular man, and commanded great respect. Due to his dismissal, the people had sentiments of hatred against the Caliph and the new Governor. This factor gave Saba ready ground to create discontent and restiveness. 'Abdullah bin Saba also found here two powerful allies in Hudaifa and Muhammad bin Abu Bakr. Both of them had grievances against 'Uthman. The former had been left an orphan in infancy. He was brought up by the Caliph. When he grew up he asked the Caliph to appoint him as Governor but 'Uthman refused to do so because he was not fit for this exalted office. He was annoyed and came to Egypt. Muhammad bin Abu Bakr owed a debt to a certain creditor who complained to the Caliph against him. The Caliph was quite impartial in his judgement. He decided the case against Muhammad bin Abu Bakr. This offended him and he joined hands with the enemies of the Caliph. 'Abdullah bin Saba took full advantage of this friction and asked the people to press 'Uthman to resign because he had usurped the right of 'Ali who deserved the Caliphate. He picked up men who lent an easy ear to what he said. He set up secret organisations in various cities. At last these organisations grew stronger and rose in open revolt against the Caliph.

THE MISCHIEF STARTS

The revolt against the Caliph started from the cantonment areas of Kufa, Basra and Fustat. At this critical juncture the Governor of Kufa, Sa'id bin al-'As left for Madinah to discuss some matters of vital importance with the Caliph. The conspirators took full advantage of his absence. Ashtar propagated that he had just returned from Madinah where Sa'id was suggesting the Caliph to decrease the pension of the soldiers of Kufa and the stipends of the women. This baseless rumour added fuel to the fire. When the news of the return of Sa'id from Madinah was received, a party of one thousand soldiers marched out from the city to block his way. Sa'id fled away in terror to seek help from the Caliph. One of his guards was killed by the rebels. A party of insurgents shadowed Sa'id and lodged a fabricated complaint to the Caliph against him. The Caliph was taken in and he dismissed the Governor. It was a blunder of the Caliph. Had he severely taken the defaulters to task, he would have crushed all the troubles brewing up against him. The mischief-mongers misconstrued this act as weakness and intensified their evil activities against the Government. Even the old Muslims could not remain immune from .their bad effects.

SEDITIONIST'S MARCH ON MADINAH

The conspirators decided to march on the Capital to present their demands. Accordingly, one thousand rebels from each province, except Syria, left for Madinah. On hearing the news of their approach, a wave of anger and fury spread through the city and the inhabitants took up their arms. The rebels were dismayed when they came to know that the people of Madinah were ready to repulse their attack unitedly. The ring leaders met the Caliph who assured them that he would redress their grievances. The mischief-mongers were satisfied and they returned. After a few days a hostile band again converged upon the Capital.

Thereupon 'Ali (may Allah be pleased with him) went towards the rebels to hold negotiations in order to pacify them. They requested 'Ali, Talha and Zubair one by one to accept their leadership, but they declined to do so. They flatly refused to become a party to their evil designs. Soon after, they produced a letter which the Egyptian band had captured from the slave of Uthman. It was alleged that the letter was addressed to 'Abdullah bin Abi Sarrah, the Governor. He was ordered to arrest, torture, cut the beards of the insurgent leaders and put them to the sword. The rebels remarked that it was a breach of promise. So they demanded the abdication of the Caliph. When 'Ali investigated the matter, the Caliph denied the truth of what they said. He stated :

> "By God, I have neither written it nor had it written for me. I have no-knowledge of it even. A counterfeit seal can also be made."

(Ibn Kathir)

'Ali at once saw through the whole game. He declared that it was a forged letter. The disruptionists had used it merely as a pretext to launch an attack on Madinah. There was no positive proof to admit that the letter was genuine. In reply to the denial by 'Uthman, mischief-mongers resumed their insolence and said, "Whether you have written this letter or some one else has written it, you are unfit for the exalted office in both the cases. You must resign at once." The aged Caliph replied, "I will never abdicate. I will never throw off the mantle which Allah has put on me. Tell me where I am wrong and I will reform myself. I am not afraid of death. I can nip the evil in the bud but I do not like shedding a drop of Muslim blood." At this time 'Uthman recalled the prophecy of the Prophet (peace and blessings of Allah be upon him) as saying :

> "O 'Uthman! Perhaps Allah may invest you with a robe of honour but, you must never take it off— (emphasised thrice).
>
> *(Tirmidhi)*

With reference to Ibn Katbir, it is narrated in *Masnad* Imam Ahmad that once the Prophet (peace and blessings of Allah be upon him) whispered something into the ears of 'Uthman and he lost colour. During the siege he uttered these sentences frequently:

> "I have made a solemn promise with the Prophet (peace and blessings of Allah be upon him) not to cause bloodshed. I shall endure all hardships with patience."
>
> *(Ibn Kathir)*

'Uthman was sure that the prophecy would turn out to be true sooner or later. The leading men of Madinah advised the rioters to retreat peacefully. But they were bent upon making mischief, they were not inclined to listen to them. Now the excitement was at its height. The rebels entered the city and became insolent and defiant of the authority of the Caliph.

GOVERNORS' CONFERENCE

At first, 'Uthman deputed some reliable companions of the Prophet (peace and blessings of Allah be upon him) to each province so that they may listen to the complaints of the people for investigations on a higher level. 'Abdullah bin 'Umar, Usama bin Zaid, Muhammad bin Muslim and 'Ammar bin Yasir were selected for this mission. He himself also called the people to Makkah at the time of the pilgrimage to redress their grievances. The disruptionists continued contriving plots against the Caliph but he tried his level best to make a peaceful settlement. 'Ammar who was despatched to Egypt did not turn up while the others held thorough enquiries of the affairs and reported that the charges were baseless. Then the Caliph summoned the Governors to meet him in Madinah after the pilgrimage. He also proclaimed that anyone who had grievances against any official might personally put it in before the Caliph. But no one stepped forward to lodge any complaint. During the conference some of the Governors suggested the Caliph to take strong measures against the conspirators but 'Uthman refused to adopt a severe attitude. Addressing the Governors, he remarked :

> "I have heard your opinions. I fear that this is the evil time foretold by the Prophet (peace and blessings of Allah be upon him). If so, I will do what I can, with all kindness and forgiveness at my command, to keep its gates shut. I will prove by my actions that I never hesitated in doing good to the people. I will not allow any blame to rest on me when I face Allah tomorrow. I am sure that the prophecy of the Prophet (peace and blessings of Allah be upon him) shall come out to be true. Allah will bestow blessings on 'Uthman if he lays down his life but does not bring the curse nearer."
>
> *(Tabaqat ibn Sa'd)*

The conference ended. The Governors departed to their respective provinces without deciding anything. Mu'awiya said, "O Commander of the Faithful! I do not think that Madinah is a safe place for you. You should better go with me to Syria". He replied, "I cannot depart from the neighbourhood of my Master (peace and blessings of Allah be upon him) even if my head is cut off". Again Mu'awiya said, "Allow me to send some troops from Syria to serve as your guard". The Caliph replied, "I do not want to create trouble in the neighbourhood of my Master (peace and blessings of Allah be upon him). I rely upon the help of my Lord".

LETTER ADDRESSED TO THE PILGRIMS

In the name of Allah Who is the Most Gracious, Most Merciful. Salutations to all the Muslims from

'Uthman, the humble servant of Allah and the Commander of the Faithful. All Praise be to Allah. There is none worthy of worship except Him. I remind you of Allah, the Great Who bestowed His blessings upon you and showed you the right path. He saved you from sedition. He sent down His Revelations to the Prophet (peace and blessings of Allah be upon him) for your guidance. He amplituded your provisions and enabled you to predominate over your opponents. So the Holy Qur'an says :

> "O ye who believe ! Observe your duty to Allah with right observance, and die not save as those who have surrendered (unto Him). And hold fast, all of you together, to the rope of Allah and do not separate. And remember Allah's favour unto you: how ye were enemies and He made friendship between your hearts so that you became as brothers by His grace; and how you were on the brink of a pit of fire and He saved you from it. Thus does Allah explain to you His Commandments that you may be guided. And there may spring from

you a body of men who should invite to goodness and enjoin right conduct and forbid evil. Such are they as are successful. And be not like those who became divided and disputed after the clear proofs had come to them. For such there is an awful punishment".

(Aale-Imran : 102-105)

"O ye who believe ! If an evil-doer brings you any news, verify it lest you should harm some folk in ignorance and then repent of what you have done. And know that among you is the Messenger of Allah; if he were to comply with your wishes in most of the matters, you would surely come to trouble; but Allah has endeared the faith to you and has beautified it in your hearts and has made disbelief and wickedness and rebellion hateful to you. Such indeed are those who follow the right course. (It is) a bounty and grace from Allah; and Allah is All-Knowing, Wise". (Al-Hujurat : 6-8)

"Lo ! Those who take a paltry price in exchange for their covenant with Allah and their oaths, they shall have no portion in the Hereafter and Allah shall never speak to them nor look upon them on the Day of Resurrection, nor will He purify them and for them shall be a grievous punishment".

(Aale-Imran : 77)

"O ye who believe ! Obey Allah, and obey the Messenger and those of you who are in authority; and if you differ in anything among yourselves, refer it to Allah and His Messenger if you are believers in Allah and the Last Day. That is best and most commendable in the long run".

(An-Nisa' : 59)

"Lo ! Those who swear allegiance unto thee (Muhammad) swear allegiance only to Allah. The Hand of Allah is above their hands. So whosoever breaketh his oath, breaketh it only to hurt his soul; while whosoever keepeth his covenant with Allah, on him will He bestow immense reward".

(12 : 90)

Allah is pleased with those who remain united. He enjoins you to avoid friction. So act upon His advice and save yourselves from the torment from which the previous sinful nations suffered. Those nations were completely disbanded and ruined due to discord and hypocrisy. In case you do not stand united, the enemy will overpower you and some of you will slander, humiliate and disgrace the others.

Thus, you will be divided into different sects. You are directed to keep in mind these verses of the Holy Qur'an :

"And O my people ! Let not your hostility towards me (Shu'aib) cause you to sin so that there befall you that which befell the folk of Nuh or the people of Hud or the folk of Salih; and the folk of Lut are not far from you. And seek forgiveness of your Lord and turn to Him (repentant). Verily, my Lord is Merciful, Most Loving."

(12 : 90)

They criticised the ruling Governors. I consulted the pious wives of the Prophet on this issue, they advised me to reinstate 'Amr bin al-'As as Governor and directed me that 'Abdullah bin Qais and Mu'awiya should work as usual as they were appointed by the previous Caliphs. I gave financial aid to the poor and the distressed as desired by the people. I provided them with the authentic text of the Holy Qur'an which was revealed to the Prophet (peace and blessings of Allah be upon him).

A group of disruptionists have risen in revolt against me. They have blocked my way to the Mosque. They have caused havoc and devastation in Madinah. They are pressing me hard for the acceptance of their demands. They want to wreak vengeance on me for my fair or foul actions. They desire that I should retire from my position. They wish that I should move to another town or province. I will never relinquish the charge of the Caliphate because I do not like to throw off the robe of honour which Allah has made me put on. I cannot tolerate parting with the place which is the burial place of my Master (peace and blessings of Allah be upon him). These people, themselves, have invested me with power. They took an oath of allegiance to me to show that they will show reverence to me and obey my just orders. Now they are bent upon the breach of faith. I have taken no drastic action against them. I dislike bloodshed and friction in the Muslim community. I request you to uphold truth and justice; and adhere to the covenant with Allah. I, hereby, absolve myself of all responsibilities. I refer my case to Allah. I seek His salvation. None can pardon except Him. Last of all, I pray to Allah that we may not indulge in impiety and debauchery.

LETTER TO THE GOVERNORS

In the Name of Allah,
the Most Gracious, the Most Merciful

Allah sent the Prophet (peace and blessings of Allah be upon him) in this world as a witness, a harbinger of glad-tidings and a warner. He acted as a summoner unto Allah and conveyed His message to the people. When his mission was accomplished, he was called to his Heavenly Home. He left the Holy Qur'an among us for guidance. Then Abu Bakr and 'Umar (may Allah be pleased with them) became his successors and rendered services in the capacity of Caliphs. After the death of 'Umar (may Allah be pleased with him), the *Majlis-e-Shura* elected me unanimously as the third Caliph not with standing the fact that I was not desirous of holding this exalted office. I acted as the disciple and follower of the Prophet (peace and blessings of Allah be upon him) and the previous Caliphs (may Allah be pleased with them). I worked to the best of my capacity and avoided innovation and formalities. The state made remarkable progress during my reign. When the hypocrites and selfish persons failed to attain undue concessions, they raked up the events of the past and raised a storm of baseless propaganda against me Out of jealousy and rancour. They charged me with certain allegations, but I endured all these absurdities with patience. I adopted no measures against them. They grew more courageous day by day and assembled in Madinah. These people bear resemblance to those who fought against the believers in the battles of Uhud and Ahzab. These people make a false show of their piety. They intend to deprive me of my life. Now help me if you like.

(Tabari, Tarihk al-Umam al-Muluk)

UTHMAN REFUTED ALLEGATIONS

On one occasion he tried to clarify his position before the leading men of Madinah as well as the ring leaders of the seditious persons. First of all he reminded the audience of his glorious services which he rendered to the cause of Islam and then he tried to rebut the allegations levelled against him. He proclaimed thus :

> “It is alleged against me that I have reserved some pastures for my personal use. By Allah, I have not done so. In these pastures graze the camels that are public property. I have not more than two camels which serve me at the time of the Pilgrimage. You are well aware of this fact that before I became Caliph, no one in Arabia possessed more camels than myself.

I am blamed that I have made alterations and additions to the Holy Qur’an. I have burnt the manuscripts. You know that the Holy Qur’an is the Last Book which was revealed to the Prophet (peace and blessings of Allah be upon him) by Allah. The companions who wrote down this Book under the supervision of the Prophet (peace and blessings of Allah be upon him) are still alive. It is they who compiled the Original Text and I despatched true copies of it to the provinces. I have burnt unauthentic manuscripts to stop all sorts of controversies.

I am accused of appointing my young, relatives as Governors. The fact is that character and ability guide my choice. Young age and relationship are not disqualifications. The officials appointed by me proved valuable assets. They rendered remarkable services to glorify Islam. It is no sin to love one's kinsmen. The Prophet (peace and blessings of Allah be upon him) has stressed to do so in many Traditions. This love has never made me unjust. As for rewards I have never given my relatives anything out of public funds. I give them presents out of my own pocket. Above all, I do not take anything from the Public Treasury for my personal expenses. The revenue of each province is spent on the public of the relevant province.

It is stated that I have given the Umayyads preference over others. This accusation is not true. But it is not a sin to belong to the Umayyad clan. The Prophet (peace and blessings of Allah be upon him) bestowed favours upon them. He made me his son-in-law. He honoured Abu Sufyan after the conquest of Makkah. He appointed him the ruler of Najran. He appointed his son Yazid the ruler of Tama'. He made Aban bin Sa'id and Khalid bin Sa'id, the Governors of Bahrain and San'a' respectively. 'Attab bin Asid worked in the capacity of the ruler of Makkah during the reign of the Prophet (peace and blessings of Allah be upon him) and the first two Caliphs (may Allah be pleased with them). Mu'awiya also occupied a prominent position during their periods.

It is said that I have allotted lands to my friends. This allegation is quite baseless. Many people from Madinah accompanied the conquering armies. Some of them settled in the subdued areas. There they acquired pieces of lands.

When the Caliph was making this speech,, Malik ibn Ashtar interrupted and created a disturbance. 'Uthman said to him, "What do you want ?" He replied, "We desire to remove you from the office of Caliphate." 'Uthman said, "I will never abdicate. I do not like to set a bad example for the generations to follow." He predicted thus : "By Allah, if you draw the sword against me, you will open among the Muslims a door of dissension that will never be closed. You will never enjoy peace and tranquillity in future. Unity and kindred among the Muslim nation shall be shattered. The Muslims will split up into different sects. Neither will you accept the leadership of one chief nor will you be able to ensue holy wars against the pagans. You will be involved in subtraction and separate Imams shall lead you in prayers."

(*Tabaqat ibn Sa'd)*

THE CALIPH WAS MALTREATED

The capital was in the grip of mutineers. The Caliph and the companions were free to attend the Mosque for daily prayers. On the Friday congregation prayers the Caliph stood on the *mimbar* (pulpit) and addressed the seditionists. He reminded them of the Prophet's curses and exhorted them to feel penitence. The reference was to the prophecy in which the Prophet (peace and blessings of Allah be upon him) had mentioned a few places and said that those encamping there, would have the curse of Allah on them. The prediction was made thus :

The Prophet (peace and blessings of Allah be upon him) said, "The armed forces stationed at the Dhi Murwa and the Dhi Khushab shall be excruciating and accursed".

(Ibn Kathir, *Al-Bidaya wal-Nihaya).*

The seditionists had actually encamped at these posts. They flew into a rage and began to stone the Caliph and the companions. Some distinguished companions such as Zaid bin Thabit and Muhammad bin Muslim were disgraced by the rebels. One man snatched the sacred reclining rod of the Prophet (peace and blessings of Allah be upon him) from the Caliph and broke it into pieces. The pious and aged Caliph was beaten mercilessly. He fell down on the ground and lost consciousness. He was removed to his house and was forbidden to enter the Mosque. The capital was full of feelings and sentiments of deep sympathy for the innocent Caliph. This state of affairs calmed the violent spirit of the mutineers and they were contented to maintain the siege around his residence instead of causing bloodshed.

THE HOUSE OF THE CALIPH WAS BESIEGED

The rebels surrounded the house of the Caliph, 'Uthman. Most of the people deserted him. The unfortunate pious soul was left alone to the tender mercies of his opponents. Only his own Umayyad kinsmen and the young ones of 'Ali, Talha and Zubair remained there to keep guard at his house. The siege continued for forty days. As the time passed, the blockade became more and more vigorous.

The rioters disallowed the supply of water to the aged Caliph. Sometimes the guards indulged in combat with the rebels. Once Hasan and Marwan were wounded in an encounter. The rioters avoided an open clash lest they should provoke the anger of Banu Hashim. During the siege 'Uthman sent 'Abdullah bin 'Abbas to lead the Pilgrimage as his deputy. The Caliph expected martyrdom at any moment. He passed his days and nights in the remembrance of Allah. He recalled to his mind the prophecy of his Master (peace and blessings of Allah be upon him) that he would face martyrdom for the sake of Allah. He was anxious to see his Master (peace and blessings of Allah be upon him) in Paradise. It is narrated by 'Abdullah bin Salam that 'Uthman said with a smiling face :

> "Tonight in the dream I have seen the Prophet (peace and blessings of Allah be upon him) in the accompaniment of Abu Bakr and 'Umar (may Allah be pleased with them) and he gave me good news that we shall have breakfast together."
>
> (Ibn Kathir, *Al-Bidaya wal-Nihaya).*

So, on Friday, he kept fast and released his prisoners. He spent his time in prayer and recitation. He continued reciting the Holy Qur'an. Although 'Uthman was sure of his martyrdom he lost no opportunity to convey the Message of Islam. Once he appeared on the roof and recited the Tradition of the Prophet (peace and blessings of Allah be upon him) as saying:

> "It is strictly prohibited to murder the Muslim brother-in-faith without three reasons, i.e., if one commits adultery in spite of being married, or one is found guilty of apostasy after embracing

Islam or one is to be slain for non-payment of ransom."

(Ibn Majah)

'Uthman solemnly proclaimed that he had never committed fornication even in the Days of Ignorance. He had not been guilty of apostasy after acceptance of Islam. He had never shed the blood of any Muslim. Last of all, he declared his belief in the Muslim creed and recited the Kalimah. *(Ibn Kathir)*

Once during the siege Umm Habiba, the wife of the Prophet (peace and blessings of Allah be upon him) decided to take some food to the Caliph but the mischief-mongers did not allow her to do so. She was soughly handled and escaped a fall only with difficulty. The rioters and insolent people showed no respect to her. Once 'Ali (may Allah be pleased with him) tried to see him but the intriguers did not permit him to do so. Off and on Zaid bin Thabit, Abu Huraira and 'Abdullah bin Zubair (may Allah be pleased with them) tried to seek permission of the Caliph to fight against the enemies of Islam but he avoided bloodshed. Some of the companions suggested that he may slip away to Makkah under the dark cover of night and seek shelter in the vicinity of the Ka'bah but he replied, "The intriguers are bent upon fighting. They will not care for the sanctity of the House of Allah. They will commit acts of sacrilege there. Although, it is prohibited to shed the blood of human beings in the Holy City yet the disruptionists, being infuriated will not refrain from doing so. I do not fear for the life which is the gift of Allah and I am ready to sacrifice it for His sake. I shall display exemplary patience in enduring all sorts of hardships."

MARTYRDOM OF 'UTHMAN (*17 June 656 A.D.*)

The mischievous activities of the rebels increased gradually. They were looking for an opportunity to enter the house of 'Uthman (may Allah be pleased with him) and put him to death. It was the time for the Pilgrimage and most of the people had left for Makkah to perform Hajj. Now the city was completely in the hands of the rebels. The small group of the defenders of the Caliph kept on resisting them. When the Pilgrimage ended, the rebels apprehended the return of the pilgrims. They decided to put into practice the nefarious design of murdering the Caliph. One night, a party of eight persons scaled the wall to the rear of the house and jumped in. Muhammad bin Abu Bakr got hold of the beard of the pious Caliph and pulled it. At this, 'Uthman said, "Had your father been alive, he would not have liked this conduct of yours." Muhammad bin Abu Bakr felt ashamed and turned aside. Then two of the rebels rushed upon the aged and humble Caliph. One of them struck an iron bar on his head while he was reciting the Holy Qur'an., The drops of his sacred blood trickled down on the following verse of the Holy Qur'an:

فَسَيَكْفِيكَهُمُ اللَّهُ ۚ وَهُوَ السَّمِيعُ الْعَلِيمُ ﴿١٣٧﴾

"And Allah will suffice thee (for defence) against them. He is the Hearer, the Knower."

(Al-Baqrah : 137)

The other struck him with his sword. Na'ila the faithful wife of 'Uthman (may Allah be pleased with her) stepped forward to shield him and she tried to avert the attack with her hand but her fingers were chopped off. 'Amru bin Hamaq inflicted nine injuries on his body with a lance and 'Umair bin Sabi kicked him to break his limbs. One of them strangled him when he was breathing his last. Two slaves of of the Caliph were also killed while defending him. So great was the terror of the rebels that for three days, the dead body of the Caliph lay unburied. At last, it was secretly buried in the cemetery of al-Baqi'. Jubair bin Mut'im led the-funeral prayers. The rebels threw the dead bodies of the slaves before the dogs. After such a dastardly act they rushed to the Public Treasury and plundered it. Lawlessness reigned over Madinah for several days.

The man with whom were married two daughters of the Prophet (peace and blessings of Allah be upon him) was killed in a miserable plight. He was the man whom Allah had promised Paradise in his lifetime. The stubborn and treacherous rebels extinguished the light which illuminated the vast Muslim Empire. 'Uthman tried his level best to prevent bloodshed even at the cost of his life. He made every effort to counter violence with love and kindness. No doubt he succeeded in his mission in the long run.

REPENTANCE OVER THE MARTYRDOM OF 'UTHMAN

The news of 'Uthman's woeful death was a rude shock to every sensible Muslim. The whole of the Muslim community expressed a deep sense of regret on his sad demise. Most of the companions of the Prophet were stunned and they burst into tears. He was a pillar on which the splendid building of Islam was resting. Those who demolished this pillar, had damaged the structure of Islam. After his cruel death, the unity of the Muslim nation was rent asunder and there was disintegration in the society.

Hudhifa said, "The assassination of 'Uthmari has caused such a breach in the edifice of Islam that the mountain will be deficient in patching it up."

Thamama bin 'Idi, the Governor of San'a' wept bitterly in a child like manner.

Abu Hamid Sa'idi said, "0 Allah ! After the assassination of 'Uthman, I make a solemn promise not to laugh till the last moment of my life."

'Abdullah bin Salam remarked, "Today the Arabs have died. The Persians have deprived them of their glory."

Abu Musa Ash'ari said, "Had the murder of Uthman been a good act, the nation would have prospered. As it was an act of sedition, it has caused bloodshed and friction."

Ali said, ''The murderers of'Uthman shall be subjected to excruciation, disgrace and the wrath of Allah, up to the Day of Resurrection."

Hadhrat A'isha (Allah be pleased with her) said, "The cruel assassins have killed an innocent and Oppressed person in cold blood. May Allah curse and revile them.",

Hassan bin Thabit' remarked, "O Abu 'Amr ! Grieve as much as you can. It is an appropriate occasion to express your lamentations. Today the towering companion of the Prophet (peace and blessings of Allah be upon him) has been slain near the Mosque just like a camel. Now he is enjoying an eternal sleep in the cemetery of al-Baqi'."

(Tabaqat Ibn Sa'd)

THE MADINITES' EVASION FROM BLOODSHED

One is naturally surprised at the indifferent attitude of the Madinites towards 'Uthman not withstanding the fact that many influential personalities like 'Ali, Talha and Zubair were present among them. Was it not their duty to defend the Caliph at the risk of their own lives? This is the question which casts a shadow of doubt upon every mind. Some historians believed that though 'Ali, Talha, Zubair and some others were not in conspiracy with the rioters yet they were against the administrative policy of 'Uthman and thus did not want to help 'him. As they were displeased with him, they kept looking on at the whole situation as disinterested observers. It is quite a misleading view. The Madinites were in every way prepared to defend the Caliph with the last drops of their blood but according to the Islamic Law they could not strike the blow first. Moreover, the rebels had not unsheathed their swords so far. There is a clear injunction of the Holy Qur'an not to take the initiative in unsheathing the sword even against the infidels. As they were Muslims, none could make the first move in shedding the blood of fellow Muslims. The Holy Qur'an says :

> "Whoso slayeth a believer deliberately, his reward is Hell for ever. Allah is wroth against him and He

hath cursed him and prepared for him an awful doom."

(An-Nisa : 93)

Similarly, the Caliph himself opposed the use of the sword and nothing could be done without his permission nor what was contrary to the clear verdict of the Holy Qur'an, which says :

"O ye who believe ! Obey Allah and obey His Messenger and those of you who are in authority."

(An-Nisa : 59)

'Ali, Talha and Zubair (may Allah be pleased with them) sent their beloved sons to defend the Caliph. They were ready to lay down their lives for his protection. Above all the rebels hesitated to take an extreme step. Apparently, it seemed that they were exerting pressure on the Caliph to resign. The Madinites were sure that the rebels would never exceed moral limits and spill the blood of the sacred Caliph.

EXONERATION OF 'ALI FROM 'UTHMAN'S MARTYRDOM

Ali and 'Uthman (may Allah be pleased with them) had a deep and sincere attachment With each other. In spite of the fact that 'Ali disliked Marwan and some other

Umayyads, he was in favour of 'Uthman from the core of his heart. His great affection and regard for Uthman is clearly manifested from this fact that he named one of his sons after the name of this saintly Caliph. He had fourteen sons and 'Uthman bin 'Ali was one of the martyrs in the tragedy of Karbala. Had he cherished anmity against him, he would never have adopted the name of 'Uthman for his son. He went one of his sons to guard the house of the Caliph. He flatly refused to support the mischief-mongers in any way. When the rioters had been using his name to fan the fire of dissatisfaction, he exhorted them to abstain from making mischief and creating rupture between him and the Caliph. When the supply of water and food to the Caliph was cut off, he went to them and said, "You are doing an evil deed. It does not behove a Muslim to tease his brother-in-faith." But this advice fell flat on them. When he set out to call on 'Uthman in compliance with his message, the rebels blocked his way and put him under house arrest in Ihjarzit, outside Madinah. The envoy of 'Uthman himself witnessed this scene. 'Ali sent his black turban to 'Uthman to show that he was quite helpless. When the time was ripe to take drastic action against the rioters, he was also besieged. After the sad demise of 'Uthman it was narrated by Abu 'Alia that 'Ali wept so bitterly that he began to hiccup. It seemed as if he would breath his last on account of this intolerable shock. It was also narrated on the authority of 'Abdullah bin 'Abbas that 'Ali proclaimed thus :

> "I am ready to declare solemnly in the House of Allah that I have no hand in the conspiracy against the life of 'Uthman. I have always forbidden the rebels but they have paid no heed to my advice."
>
> *(Al-Bidaya wal-Nihaya)*

Some of the critics maintained why the murderers were not severely dealt with if the hands of 'Ali were clear of the stains of blood of the sacred Caliph. 'Ali intended to take revenge for the murder of his companion but the shade of anarchy and lawlessness prevailed in every hook and corner of the state. This state of affairs prevented him from taking immediate action. Moreover, the murder of 'Uthman was hot the mischief of a few individuals who could 'be easily captured and executed. There were a large number of men at the back of this conspiracy. It was an uphill task to deal with. Uthman himself hesitated to wield the sword against the disruptionists. Such a step may be sure to lead to a dangerous conflagration.

UTHMAN'S REIGN AND ADMINISTRATION

During the first six years of the Caliphate of 'Uthman (may Allah be pleased with him) the Muslim State progressed by leaps and bounds. The power of Islam was at the climax of its glory. After the suppression of anarchy in some provinces a vast territory including Turkistan, Khurasan, Armenia, Azarbaijan and Cyprus, was annexed to the State of Islam. 'The Muslims also established a sway on the sea during the first naval operations in the History of Islam. During his reign the machinery of the Government worked exactly on the lines of the previous Caliphs of Islam. There was absolutely no change in the system of Government which had a democratic pattern. The "Council of Advisers *(Majlis-e-Shura)* was maintained and all affairs were settled by it. The position of the Caliph was just like a commoner. Being a ruler he was considered to be the servant of his nation. He was accessible to every one. ' He led a simple life and kept no guards to protect him. The Caliph kept himself fully aware of the state of affairs. Every complaint against the Governor or any other official was reviewed with full attention and prompt action against the defaulters was taken without any consideration of his status. The Revenue Department was established and it worked in a more flourishing way. The stipends were awarded to widows, orphans and deserving persons. 'Uthman tried his best to root out ignorance from the country. He made special arrangements for the teaching of the Holy Qur'an. He gave reasonable stipends to the teachers, scholars and capable students to encourage them. He completed many works of public utility. The roads were repaired and new ones constructed. Many rest houses for travellers were built. The Police Headquarters and Stations were set up so that the people might live in peace. Their lives and property might remain safe and protected. The frontiers Were fortified and several military posts were established. 'Uthman created new posts in the Army and appointed deserving persons to them. He prepared a big naval force and trained it fully to fight sea battles.

There was a scarcity of water in Arabia. He had new wells dug and improved the condilion of the existing fountains. Many bridges were built. During his reign the courtyard of the Ka'bah was extended and new Mosques were built. He had the Mosque of the Prophet expanded and decorated. As agriculture and trade progressed, he set up new markets and business centres. Pastures to breed horses and camels were reserved.

The reign of 'Uthman began with popular enthusiasm but due to the attitude of some of his kinsmen, doubts and suspicions were created in the hearts of the people and thus they revolted against authority. Most of his kith and kin acquired nearly all the profitable key positions in the Government and the other tribes grew jealous of them. The Caliph had full faith in his relatives and he ignored the others. Had he depended upon all the loyal elements among the companions and the chiefs of the other tribes, regardless of their clan affiliations, he could have organised a strong Central Government to overcome any political crisis.

'UTHMAN'S CHARACTER

'Uthman (may Allah be pleased with him) was a renowned companion of the Prophet (peace and blessings of Allah be upon him). He was his true devotee. He scrupulously followed in his footsteps. He was well known for his chastity, integrity and modesty. He was gifted with a pure nature since his birth but Islam had a deep edifying influence on it. He was always afraid of the wrath of Allah. He never acted against the teachings of the Holy Qur'an and the Sunnah of his Master (peace and blessings of Allah be upon him). He was extremely kind-hearted. He was lenient towards the guilty even for fear of aggression. During the Caliphate he in person conducted the obligatory prayers in the Mosque and was regular even in his midnight prayers. When he got up at night, he never disturbed his servants for his own comforts. He did all his work with his own hands. Although he had attained old age, yet he was constant in keeping fast. He was generous at heart. He spent money lavishly for the welfare of the poor. Although he was wealthy, he wore simple dress and ate plain food. He prohibited his wife to dress herself in costly costume. She performed her house-hold duties herself. He never displayed niggardliness. Riches had no fascination for him. When the Muslims were in very straitened circumstances, he rendered financial services to the cause of Islam. Although a reasonable amount was duly sanctioned from the Public Treasury to meet the personal expenses of the Caliph, he drew nothing.

Modesty was the most salient feature of his' character, even. Even the angels envied his modesty. He had never nude, even, in loneliness and his knees seldom remained uncovered when he was sleeping or sitting. He had a weakness for his relatives and brethren-in-faith. He often fargave his staunch opponents. He was always inclined to overlook faults in people. He did not believe in retaliation.

Some critics accused him of weakness of determination and lack of courage. But it is a wrong supposition. A man who could face the mighty Empire of Rome and Persia would certainly have been a man of high courage. A man who did not submit before the pressure of the disruptionists and sacrificed his life obeying the orders of his Master, would surely be a personality with resolute and firm character. He could have smashed the rebels easily but he avoided bloodshed. The courage and faith displayed by him have few parallels in history. He was besieged by his sworn enemies. Death stared him in the face but he welcomed death with a smiling face because it would send him to a grave in Madinah and Paradise. He prized the neighbourhood of his Master over all things. No power could separate him from Madinah where the Prophet (peace and blessings of Allah be upon him) lay in eternal rest. This death was dearer to 'Uthman than life outside Madinah. He had a firm faith in the prophecy of the Prophet (peace and blessings of Allah be upon him) who had predicted a period of lawlessness and unrest in the wake of prosperity. It was narrated on the authority of 'Uthman (may Allah be pleased with him) that his Master (peace and blessings of Allah be upon him) awoke one night. He was much worried and looked dejected. He said :

> "Glory be to Allah ! What great treasures He has awarded my followers and what an unrest has accompanied the immense riches."

From the beginning of the restlessness, 'Uthman (may Allah be pleased with him) felt sure that the terrible calamity was inevitable and it must descend. He tried to delay it with politeness and forgiveness. He thought that violence would bring disaster and friction. He kept in mind another prophecy of the Prophet (peace and blessings of Allah be upon him) It said, "When the sword is once out among my followers, it will remain thus till the Last Day." 'Uthman, being a true devotee and follower of the Prophet (peace and blessings of Allah be upon him) and did not order his faithful and strong army to unsheathe their swords lest this action should shatter the solidarity of Islam. He proved himself to be a worthy follower to the Prophet (peace and blessings of Allah be upon him) and a beacon light to the following generations to remain united.

IMPARTIALITY IN THE SELECTION OF GOVERNORS

The main allegation levelled against 'Uthman was the appointment of his young relatives as Governors. No doubt he had appointed some of his young and capable kinsmen as Governors but they proved themselves valuable assets. They distinguished themselves as conquerors and administrators. Their remarkable victories and achievements justify their selection on their own merits and absolve 'Uthman of any proclivities. He removed the Governor whenever any complaint was lodged against him. He did so regardless of any consideration for his relationship. The Governor of Syria, Mu'awiya, was a near relative of the Caliph but his appointment was made by 'Umar (may Allah be pleased with him). Sa'd, the Conqueror of Persia, was also appointed as the Governor of Kufa by 'Umar (may Allah be pleased with him). He was replaced by Mughira on the basis of a minor complaint against him. When 'Umar (may Allah be pleased with him) was on his death-bed, he directed 'Uthman (may Allah be pleased with him) to reinstate him. He acted upon his advice and replaced Mughira by Sa'd. When Walid, the Governor of Kufa, was accused of drinking wine, he was not only dismissed but actually awarded the prescribed number of stripes according to the Islamic Law. Had 'Uthman (may Allah be pleased with him) been really actuated by any motives of relationship, he could really have managed to shield him. 'Abdullah bin 'Amir was also a relative of 'Uthman but his achievements in the reconquest of Persia and subjugation of vast territory furnish a solid proof that his selection was made purely on the basis of merit. But he was also sacked when the insurgents did not like him. It is quite evident that the charge of partiality against 'Uthman was absolutely baseless. It was a mere pretext to spread dissatisfaction against the pious Caliph. His character was perfectly free from the blemish of nepotism and partiality.

FAVOURABLE TRADITIONS OF THE PROPHET REGARDING 'UTHMAN

1. It is narrated on the authority of Abu Sa'id that once the Prophet (peace and blessings of Allah be upon him) kept on praying for 'Uthman (may Allah be pleased with him) from dusk to dawn. He repeatedly said, "O Allah ! I am pleased with 'Uthman. I beseech Thee to be pleased with him."
2. It is narrated on the authority of Abu Sa'id that the Prophet (peace and blessings of Allah be upon him) said, "Uthman ! Allah has reprieved you of all the sins committed by you."
3. It is narrated by Jabir that once a certain person requested the Prophet (peace and blessings of Allah be upon him) to lead the, funeral prayers of the one deceased. He declined to do so. The companions were much surprised. One of them asked him the reason for refusal. He said that the attitude of the deceased was hostile towards 'Uthman and Allah was displeased with him for this enmity."

(Tirmidhi)

4. It is narrated by Talha that the Prophet (peace and blessings of Allah be upon him) said, "Every

Messenger of Allah shall have a companion in Paradise and my close associate in Paradise shall be 'Uthman bin 'Affan."

(Masnad Ahmad)

5. It is narrated on the authority of Abu Musa Al-Ash'ari that once the Prophet (peace and blessings of Allah be upon him) was sitting near the well in the company of 'Umar and Abu Bakr (may Allah be pleased with them). His knees were naked. In the meantime 'Uthman (may Allah be pleased with him) happened to come there. At once the Prophet (peace and blessings of Allah be upon him) covered the knees and said, "Even the angels of Allah envy the modesty of 'Uthman but the nation will disregard him. I, however, give him the glad tidings of Paradise." *(Darimi)*

6. It is narrated by Hadhrat 'A'isha (may Allah be pleased with her) that one day the Prophet (peace and blessings of Allah be upon him) had wrapped himself in my coverlet. He was lying on the bed. Suddenly Abu Bakr (may Allah be pleased with him) came, held some conversation and left. Then 'Umar (may Allah be pleased with him) called on him and departed after a short stay. Then followed 'Uthman (may Allah be pleased with him). No sooner did he step in the Prophet (peace and blessings of Allah be upon him) became cautious and set his clothes

right. He sat for a while and went away. After his departure, she asked him the reason for becoming so careful with regard to dress. He replied that 'Uthman was extremely modest. Had he not done so, he would not have uttered even a word due to bashfulness.

(Mishkat)

7. It is narrated on the authority of Ibn 'Umar (may Allah be pleased with him) that the Prophet (peace and blessings of Allah be upon him) said, "I saw a balance tonight. I was made to sit in one of its pans and all my adherents were put in the other. My pan was heavier than that of the latter. Similarly, Abu Bakr, 'Umar and 'Uthman (may Allah be pleased with them) were weighed. They were heavier (in virtues) than all the people of the Muslim Community."

(Ibn Kathir, *Al-Bidaya wal-Nihaya)*

SOME OUTSTANDING ATTRIBUTES OF 'UTHMAN

1. He was the fourth among the malo converts.
2. He was the first to migrate among the followers of the Prophet (peace and blessings of Allah be upon him).

3. He had the distinction of becoming an emigrant twice. At first, he migrated to Abyssinia and then to Madinah.

4. He earned the title of *Dhun-nurain* because he had the honour of entering into matrimonial alliance with two daughters of the Prophet (peace and blessings of Allah be upon him). These daughters were the lights which illuminated his house. Thus he was called the possessor of two lights.

5. His character was free from the blemish of theft, adultery, drinking and gambling even during the Days of Ignorance.

6. 'Uthman (may Allah be pleased with him) had so much regard for the Prophet (peace and blessings of Allah be upon him) that till his death he had never touched the private part of his body with the hand which he used in taking the oath of allegiance to the Messenger of Allah (peace and blessings of Allah be upon him).

7. He was the person in whose favour a few verses of the Holy Qur'an were revealed.

8. He was the exalted man for whom the *Bai'at al-Ridwan* took place. He was given the gladtidings of Paradise in his lifetime. The Prophet (peace

and blessings of Allah be upon him) in person took a similar vow of fealty on behalf of 'Uthman (may Allah be pleased with him) and proclaimed, "My hand is the hand of 'Uthman." This revealed the esteem in which he held him.

9. He was elected Caliph on the consensus of Muslim opinion.

10. 'Uthman (may Allah be pleased with him) authenticated and fully affirmed the prophecy of the Prophet (peace and blessings of Allah be upon him) :

    "Chosroes and Caesar once squandered shall never rise to power again."

11. He was one of the scribes of the Prophet (Peace and blessing of Allah be upon him) to write down portions of Qur'an as they were revealed.

12. He put an end to the controversy and disparity in respect of the recitation of the Holy Qur'an.

13. Above all, courage, endurance and patience were his special attributes. The event of his martyrdom bears similitude to the incident relating to the two sons of Adam. The Holy Qur'an describes it thus:

"But recite to them with truth the tale of the two sons of Adam (Habil and Qabil), how each of them offered sacrifice, and it was accepted from the one and it was not accepted from the other. The one said, "I will certainly kill you." The other replied, "Allah accepteth (sacrifice) only from those who are Allah-conscious. Even if you stretch your hand against me to kill, I shall never stretch my hand against you to kill. Verily ! I fear Allah, the Lord of the Worlds. Lo ! I would rather you should bear the punishment of the sin against me and your own sin and become one of the dwellers of the Fire. That is the reward of evil-doers."

(Al-Maidah : 27-29)

No doubt, the martyrdom of the innocent Habil was glorious but that of 'Uthman (may Allah be pleased with him) was crowned with, much more dignity. Perhaps Habil lacked in resources of power but 'Uthman (may Allah be pleased with him) had the full ruling force at his command. When the swords of the opponents were want only dangling round his face, he fulfilled the promise made with the Prophet (peace and blessings of Allah be upon him) and endured all the hardships with patience. He sacrificed his life for the sake of Allah without causing bloodshed among the Muslims.

SOME GLORIOUS SAYINGS OF 'UTHMAN

1. Whosoever becomes fully aware of the world, abhors it.
2. One who loves Allah loves solitude.
3. Do not make others to shoulder your responsibilities, light or heavy.
4. Charity is the fruit of riches, good deeds are the outcome of knowledge and pleasure of Allah is the reward of sincerity.
5. Most excellent is the faith of a man who enjoys the company of the pious.
6. Useless is the Mosque where the prayers are not offered and rewardless is the prayer which is not offered in the Mosque.
7. Bootless is a good opinion which is not acted upon and purposeless is a long life in which virtuous deeds are not done to serve as provisions for the Hereafter.
8. One should not subdue oneself to circumstances, however destitute one may be.
9. Deal with the people and you will find them just like venomous creatures.

10. Whosoever does not recognize the rights of human beings, does not recognize the rights of Allah.

11. Sins lead to perturbation.

12. Whosoever is fond of rich dishes, should always keep in mind that his body has to serve the purpose of diet in the next world.

INDEX